The Ditch Was Lit Like This

The Ditch Was Lit Like This

Sean Johnston

thistledown press

© Sean Johnston, 2011
All rights reserved

No part of this publication may be reproduced or transmitted in any form or by any means, graphic, electronic or mechanical, including photocopying, recording, or any information storage and retrieval system, without permission in writing from the publisher or a licence from The Canadian Copyright Licensing Agency (Access Copyright). For an Access Copyright licence, visit www.accesscopyright.ca or call toll free to 1-800-893-5777.

Thistledown Press Ltd.
118 - 20th Street West
Saskatoon, Saskatchewan, S7M 0W6
www.thistledownpress.com

Library and Archives Canada Cataloguing in Publication
Johnston, Sean, 1966-
The ditch was lit like this / Sean Johnston.

Poems.
ISBN 978-1-897235-94-2

I. Title.

PS8569.O391738D58 2011   C811'.6   C2011-905351-9

Cover and book design by Jackie Forrie
Printed and bound in Canada

 Canada Council for the Arts Conseil des Arts du Canada   SASKATCHEWAN ARTS BOARD   Canadian Heritage Patrimoine canadien

Thistledown Press gratefully acknowledges the financial assistance of the Canada Council for the Arts, the Saskatchewan Arts Board, and the Government of Canada through the Book Publishing Industry Development Program for its publishing program.

This book is for everywhere and everyone I come from. The next one is for Janeen.

Contents

10	Drumheller
12	The Complicated Mawkishness of My Daily Walk Home
13	December 12, 2007
16	This Morning
17	Descending into Calgary
18	Obviously
19	The Painting by the Door
20	Storm Windows
21	Postcard from Asquith
22	Ghazal
23	August
26	Dead Song
27	Fend
29	We're All Invited
33	Finally
34	Last Summer in Rosetown
35	City Hospital, Saskatoon
36	Nothing Broken
37	Progress Report
38	Autobiography and the Machine
42	Night Clouds
44	Ghazal
45	A Black and White Photograph
46	Blue
47	Today a Blue Bowl
48	Bull Island

50	December
52	The Arrangements
53	Asquith 18 km
54	That Old Silver Ford
55	Green Lawn, Under the Trees, a Cemetery Across the Street
56	Still Life, Fixing the Mazda Pickup
59	Ghazal for Ross Leckie
60	Second Opinion
62	Seattle
63	This Is a False False Mark
66	Prairie Realism
67	Ghazal
68	God Help Me
69	They Meet Each Other in Airports
70	Snow Storm on Nose Hill
71	How Are We Betrayed?
72	My Case
73	With His New Tooth
76	Hinge
77	What Is the Best Thing To do On A Hot Summer Day, Stopped For Road Construction?
80	Plain Truck
81	With My Own Shovel
83	Ghazal for John Newlove
84	If You Look
85	February 15, 2009
88	The Final Poem
89	1984 F150

when it's night, because it is

Drumheller

The sun. A dog.
The page leaks onto the poem.
A heart unloads more heat.

Yesterday the asphalt came apart
and showed the world underneath.

Today everything turns
like a top in oil. There is still air.

Yesterday the old man, with his famous
stooped body, rode the heatwaves
to Saskatoon and back again.

Today there is a prophet we don't see,
according to legend. He does not sweat.
He holds a hoodoo pebble in his hand.

Tomorrow, this arrangement comes
to an end. Tomorrow and the day after it.
The inverted air will breathe its sin
and everyone, I among them,

will pray for someone in a dreamcoat,
or a beard. But Jesus will not come.
We will drink our coffee and prepare for
whatever it is, pounding nails into wood all day.

And the women in our life will never speak.
The dog will breathe without a sound.
The sun remains.

This page is out of my hands.
The unspooled heart flicks like the tongue of a snake.
Are you ready?

The Complicated Mawkishness of My Daily Walk Home

Schools of painted wooden fish are stitched with wire to this wire fence

so children seem as natural as the weeds and rubble

the fence encloses. The beauty of the neighborhood

is everyone's business, so that's why my child

hung a blue fish on there with eyes as perfect as conjoined

moons, after a drought, above a dying fire. Choking, wordless,

he hides all day in his room. I can't believe

he stutters but I hear it sometimes

when there are strangers at the table. Everything he does

is in these projects, when he's silent, in the winter

or summer colour he chooses, his precise decisions. He never stencils,

and that's why I can't abide the stupid orange fish beside his,

the one with nothing but that white LILY, standing out, here,

far from the ocean, as if a fish were an orange, as if

water weren't blue as night, when it's night,

because it is.

December 12, 2007

Was there a time when light was in
divisible, parted neither by skin or this
tree setting its clock—
                    I slept soundly
as I could just to meet
the morning whole

                    —you see my point: I was not
whole.
    —no lesson, that's the lesson, or the lesson is
we can live without our limbs, without the bodies of our brothers
                  because they are dead because they
die.
        That's the circular logic the
                        deserted mind submits
to the heart, knowing it is
faulty, saying only, this is
the latest intelligence:
        they are dead because they die and we will die too, but not
before we have run through all of this again, everything caught like
water eroding rock and
        deeper as if / and   oh:

when I fell—moving him from his wheelchair to the couch—
did I do more damage
                than I thought?

    why could I not have fallen
the other way, had him fall on me as I did
one summer day on a slow ride up from

the river when he was young and light and my
wet shoes slipped and the bike was falling
and all that happened that day
was my torn shin and him laughing above me because he could not move
                                            on his own,
because of his condition, his elaborately miswired body,
and I laughed too and breathed

   so one morning he was dead and I wanted out of my own body too
quickly because it could not hold
                                          it was not holding it
was emptying and why
was this mountain beside me and why was I
not next door and how does a man
keep working when all he ever believed in
was work and what makes it true

                        that a man has to sit and talk about
his brother with his body there in the room?
and what makes it true that he can't keep hammering in stakes and
building more roads? and what makes it true
that his body will be gone too
                              and all he can do is stare and
make dry noises when people come by to shake his hand?

                     I mean I know he's dead but *you* cannot
say that about him. I was the one who had to press down on his chest
to be sure.

         But when our brothers are dead they recede and in this dark
bar I want no more of the chatter of labour, the hardware of winter,
the wet laughter of children who've earned one paycheque and
learned one joke—

and the thank you that bloomed for the words of our talking—we
agreed: nothing small will happen:

                now:

these small giants that are pressing down upon the earth,
                          this entire seed bag thrown and
flourishing—I have been told recently
                some people think to move or vice versa. I move to
write or write to move to think.

                I heard of a [doctor] / *who if he only says their name*
and so on. And I have been told
                my entire life, in so many words, go down to the
river, get down to the river to be saved
                and light will
enter your heart and shine.

I believe I have made my way as I could.
                I walked all over the river;
where is the wet heart working its way
                          in the dark? Where is its
opposite also, its dry radical its drowning its cold killing air its work
with the enemy its deliberate opening its blooming rupture its
tumour on our lips its remarkable light that was here one morning
  I am sure?

This Morning

I feel our blood
warm and flesh stretch
and sleep again.

I don't remember all the lies that I told,
but I remember why I told them.

Descending into Calgary

The moral of flight is not clear. Here,
between day and night, arguments

occur. Hide. Your sins are not yet forgiven
whether you dart quickly or glide. Forget

the wheel, remember the sky, remember
its properties, its weightless stretch between days—

the blue-furred hills that forget in the dark
and mimic light by holding onto shadow

that surely, by now, is unnecessary. Please
step off the plane privately, despite touching

strangers and avoiding their baggage
and smiling at those just leaving the cockpit

where they must be as anxious as you
just to get through your tube and by

the hard floors and past your last doors,
into the air to breathe the dark sky.

Obviously

Obviously, the moon and its shadows,
the moon and what it did, the moon
and its movement with water—

I said it to her, fresh as we were,
I said it to her because the night
had already happened, and the dark,

and we'd missed it and then the moon
with its sudden appearance made sudden
by our muscled ignorance, our concern

with other concerns—the sex, for instance;
the noise of it and would it be wrapped
up properly or would a baby wake up

and announce itself, our baby just next
door, in such a room—and it didn't and so
suddenly, the moon, and I said it to her

and of course, she said to me, of course.

The Painting by the Door

There is nothing to it. It's a plain at night.

But you're right. There *is* something:
it's a wolf unhappy with being seen.

There are tracks that in the morning
will be gone. And stars leave a glow,

of course, on the snow. We're not even
here, of course, except now. It could be

about anything, an unwrapped ankle, swollen
lakes—but you're right. It's about

this kind of wolf, on this kind of night.

Storm Windows

Given that the history of love begins
now, I wake up early to water my lawn in the dark,
where the sprinkler's ministrations of the air are distorted quietly
by the lightening of the sky.
                                       When I could not
substantiate the claims I made I knew the world was lying
to my body. I knew this in the way the little ocean knows it's time
to retreat again, but for how long? And why?

If the onus were reversed, and I had to prove to the earth how
straight my heart would shoot if only it weren't stupid and blind,
cripes, I would be gone before I began,
                                        laughing like someone said
cock in church, rolling on the ground in love with my anatomy
like when I was a boy, or just yesterday night when I couldn't believe
the air was so fresh
        and the astonished windows
                        and the curious sky
pressing through the roof

    But the onus is on this oblivious planet out the door, not me, and its work proceeds; it spits out glottal myths and declares all the time with its sun and its wind and our hero touching bushes that sing, our hero touching a rusting axe with his forehead and singing himself, if that is a song, and it is, our hero singing then, our hero singing, and our hero singing and we are oblivious because we don't know the words but here it comes again, the friend of a friend of a friend of the hero, and she's humming quietly in the dark with her lips to our heart.

Postcard from Asquith

Well, there is little to say.
This prairie road makes my heart
into a legend and the fantastic
land you are from holds my thoughts
tonight. I can be forgiven
for not believing, on this thin highway,
in mountains, or in the ocean.

I picture you, hands out, palms up,
before a wood cabin, smiling in love
with all that's hidden. Your empty hands
a delicate reminder; nothing, actually,
can be made.

This is as close as I can get—
I saw a narwhal on television
and I know you
could name it.

Ghazal

For the last time, the boy stands in his boots
crying to the sky, mittenless and red.

Ignore it, she said, shouldering her bag
and walking fast. Her eyes are the fulcrum.

A hammer's journey is concentric to
its owner's heart, I hope. We believe.

I am on my way in the dark. Prayers
follow me and old hinges nudge gates.

Laid out dark beside a wet hole on the prairie,
my father. Grow a fast tree for shade.

August

A river winds
            round us.
                        Slurring cars
ride voices
            stretched through
                        rainy streets.
A shadow moves
            beside you,
                        a slow blink
in off-white
            sheets. Our glass
                        door moves,
almost closing
            each time I am
                        awake. The dark
asphalt is
            clear, everywhere,
                        in reflected air.
It shines, a
            syllabus of quick
                        wounds. Nothing
small happens.
            Hope will
                        believe in

itself, if
                nothing else.
                                We breathe in
the threat of
                new rain through
                                open windows and
rivers and gardens
                redress calmly
                                just now.

the ditch was lit like this

Dead Song

We walked one night, leaning
each to the other, through a city graveyard.
She was singing the song
we'd been singing all day.

There is something dead here,
I said, *try not to sing.*

And her throat,
where moments ago had been song,
coaxed less than a voice into air.
Her lips formed my name

and me, I had forgotten
my momentary caution, and kissed her
then, like all the dead were living.

Fend

A prairie bus cannot forget.
The plane. A car.
                Why
these moments, in the dark,
half-asleep against cool glass
my heart cannot get larger.

              And
whatever has happened, in these
cramped seats, to shorten my words,

the humility with which I approach
long words, complex breath, is false,
of course; marred by both fear
and contempt, as the mother's chattering
across the aisle to a boy who would sleep,
if only he could, if only she would
let him be, to word his first journey
himself, in dreams, is also informed
by fear she pretends is only for the child,
by contempt she wants to believe is only born
of a world that could do what has been done
to the boy, and not to her own spinning heart,
which cancels out absence over and over again,
by throwing out words that grow larger and larger;
the only thing blunt, the boy, his small face
untouched by words, clean and exhausted.

And beside these two characters,
me, riding to you, not afraid
of large words – you know my heart, not a flash,
an elaborate flourish. At dawn
a dog barks outside in the dark.

We're All Invited

> *Do not say the moment was imagined*
> *Do not stoop to strategies like this*
>   — Leonard Cohen

While the pale moonlight lit the ditch, the ditch was lit like this:

I was a child once more—I mean I wanted
to plead. Of course, there is always a man with a guitar
somewhere

and the response is either love returned or love withheld—that is,
of course, if something has been risked, and the real invitation
is this: birth,
                eyes that behold beauty,
                              hearts that move toward it.

The problem is that every gesture is an invitation—a smile
in a public place—say a garden, on a dull day—and next thing
you know you're climbing her wall to sing.
                                And what for? To give her
your own invitation, a tiny memory from your childhood,
to make her sad? or show you have a heart? Who knows?
    But you're eager for another story—one that shows her also
childlike.

      Even a simple description traces the movement of
                                    the eye, either up
to somewhere higher, or from somewhere up

                                    there, down to where
we stand. You see,

the lawn is a document of
a life we would lead if
we were grass. It's short and green, cut
weekly as it reaches for the sky—but here
                              we are again: the sky is too
ambitious for such small beings
who stand in groups and grow.

So, it is short and green, cut weekly as it reaches up,
                                        just up.

So, after the singing, after the stories, we spent
money together, we went swimming at
midnight on the highway's edge of town,
in the little pool by
the motel office porch light.   After a while,
                              all invitations are made
silently, in a routine that resembles a novel disintegrating
during the first world war (not the pages, not the binding, but
the words and their thoughts—
the page become white space, littered with
typed objects
              and meaning accrues, of course, in
the spaces, which were not littered, but did
the littering). It isn't doubt they
bring, it is possibility, an illumination that joins
the figures on a page. I am almost

as old as my grandfather when
he died of a faulty heart. He was
a pitcher, a farmer, a sunny disposition I know
too little of. Ten years ago I drove my truck into
a field of summer fallow after two months of too little
sleep, after two months of praying for rain, of praying for
a day off. The machines all worked half a mile away,
pulling a new highway from the ditches of
the old and I was on my back in the sunshine asleep.

I was not afraid of anything in
the air, in the grey dirt, in the blue above, in
my dying of my own faulty heart. That night
I told the collector on the phone no. Just because
you say I owe. I don't.

We have all been summoned, politely, innocently, to our end—

                    Look at the pennies on the floor. Look
for your holed elbows, your wet cuffs, your darned
toes that still leak.
              Who cares?
                        Your skin doesn't.

Leak, I mean.
        Leak in, at least.
                Everything falls out.

If I were to be honest, I am
tired of love songs and high end emotions
that churn little people into big, at night

especially. The dark horse wins at night when
our imagination is a Hollywood imitation no matter how hard we
try to begin with white space and return to
our first memory.
     Okay, begin from
that first absence. One day the sun does nothing
but flatter; next thing you know
you're sorting each other's pills.

This is how to get away from spending all you've got
on these new emotive machines that slicken
the grime. It's a lie.

   Everything falls out.

And it's true: When the pale moonlight lights
the ditch, the ditch is lit like this.

Finally

mouths open
like pores relaxing
at night asking
questions. Strong
words, they agree,
strong words and
they wait, lungs
breathing air.
Shadings trapped
in shelter. Wind
wheels outside
and glass waits.
Listen. We are
already inventing
flesh from bone.
Night air
wrestling
alone.

Last Summer in Rosetown

Every afternoon he said
a thing to make her blush.
She scolded him, my grandmother

did, with a smile: his body
was too stooped to be as young
as she imagined herself. His hands

long unused to delicacy, his
fingers were too thick for switches.
He courted her, half-believing in

the world she was slipping into,
half in the world that would not
let him lift her from her chair

into her bed. She stunned him
the first time she said bluntly
he was moving too fast, slow down.

But he could not leave the room as
quickly, and heard her tell the nurse
*I really like this new man, but
it's way too soon to marry.*

City Hospital, Saskatoon

He's blind from watching her sleep
as he leaves into dark
and starts home.

At the door, a woman, working
the new shift, her mouth
open in a smile.

It swims against the darkness of this
night; not a miracle
but a clue, and he

feels like a thief, surprised
at the sudden glory
in his heart.

The lights in the parking lot show
pools of naked asphalt kept
pale yellow when

the sun is down. A midnight spark
glints off the key as he
opens his car door.

Everything still turns. Still standing,
he looks into the dark, waiting,
at least, for fear.

But the black beginning of a new day
brings clean air into his lungs.

Nothing Broken

The hood of my car closed five years ago
on my left hand. January in Ottawa is cold enough.
I was preserved. *Does this hurt?*
the doctor asked two hours later.

We agreed the nerve damage helped.
I said it was a little funny and she smiled.
Maybe I have a reputation. I am known,
perhaps, for my hyperbole, but people moaned,

screamed and cried from hidden injuries.
Their bodies were smooth under clean sheets.
This is awkward, I thought. No broken bones
to show my neighbour, after the anxious drive,

the dinner left on the stove. I have no
money to pay for the gas, just two
normal hands, one numb and washed,
a bloody dishrag in the other.

Progress Report

These things have happened so far:
    I built this world of gesture and impulse;
    I walked into a wall and thus made real my body;
    she questioned my motives, but left the door unlocked;
    the hearse collided with a truck;
    I hit the ground holding the coffin above me;
    my legs were sore, my arms were sore;
    nobody was laughing at my jokes—

These things will happen tomorrow or the next day:
    I will find a way out of here;
    my body will be a paper flag;
    the things I've imagined will be real;
    I will die for lack of fuel;
    I will brush up against you and whisper a warning;
    a word will make dust of bone and hair—

These things I know:
    my own heart; a glass wall.

Autobiography and the Machine

1

He worked by himself, on his
specific corner of the machine. His heart became
heavier than the hearts of the others, he thought.
Because he became Canadian quietly,
dodging situations that might compromise
the security of his war, there were those
who mistook him for an idiot savant—
a book-reader who chuckled to himself
at nothing, or shadows.

Perhaps the other Canadians are marrying
each other in the machine's courtyard, or
perhaps they embrace in celebration of some
contest:
        This is glorious!
                                            he thought,
and turned, smiling, back to his mad work.

2

They tell me don't forget this was once
a stream of cold mountain water, don't forget
this was once water.

The dog at my heels, with no one left to guide,
sniffs for junk in my shoes. They are
this close to calling the whole thing off.
Don't forget this was once a mountain.

3

In the custom of Canadians I muttered some words
and closed the car door. Ensconced in my capsule.

Already today I've had one glass of milk,
two cups of coffee and a small sip of water
with my pill. And I am washed, rinsed, and
dried. Thank God.

4

Remember this:

> the others you see are paper
>
> the machine is just a ruse
>
> do your part

5

Time to start again. Try first with a new
outfit. *Some kind of cowboy stopped by
the house while you were out. I said you were
hunting. He said he would wait.*

Where is he?

6

One more time. I've become Canadian. I am
not ashamed. My horrible secret is this:
the machine is just a ruse—it conceals
a device.

7

I still remember the mountain, the stream,
the green beside and its scent. I want to be
where they marry each other.

The device hurts itself—a perpetual engine
cancered out with giddy, imploding teeth.
Listen:

8

If he were honest he would drop to his knees
days and nights, by the corner of the concealing
machine, and ask, and say, and thank.

He and his tool kit—they tape-up
ideal words like *bliss*,

and send them into the wild again.

9

All the buildings and motors are blistered and
peeling. The Prime Minister is on TV
asking for our patience in some new code.

Numbers beget numbers and silence.

Looking out the corner of my eye, I wish
he would seem more nervous—we could all
gather and let him know:

Don't worry, and

We're still working, and

There will be a device in my lifetime.

10

A black suit and tie, hard shoes on concrete.

He shakes his head and takes his hat off.

The slicked-back hair on his head doesn't move.

11

The time has come.

Brush the lint off your clothes and take a quick walk, just to get loose.

Here is a breath

                       the jarred-up surface of

the world is breaking.

12

It isn't locked.

It just won't open.

Night Clouds

This brushed fog cannot be real.
The bills have been paid. But even
in dark, they cloud the sky:

a cold metal case in the wet
night, with a slick film
over it as in a child's book

of anatomy. But the scarred
moon reveals, now and again, the dirty
little smudges where it was

once clear. The air seems to cling
to us. It's the work of the unreal
clouds. And we slow with each

breath.

what the son is accused of

Ghazal

A documentary plunges into it
on television. Falling is mistaken for flight.

Come here and tell me about your day,
she says, her knifeless hands kindling air.

Linger in the room, and light, wordless
remarks become shy come-ons.

Friends, I would like to read you a lyric.
It's about now and the sound of plates and cups.

Rust plays its artless tune on the car parked
in the grass. Sunlight and rust.

A Black and White Photograph

where in summer,
the boy of me holds a gopher
limp in both hands.

Beside the boy, grinning,
an uncle leans a rifle straight
in the necessary silence.

His hand is on the boy's head,
his arm in line with the horizon
at the height of a child—

the boy silent also, not knowing
how to behave; solemn, perhaps,
held in the heart of the frame.

So little blood from the animal.
The gun is straight and the blue above
depends forever on the possible

sound in its throat.

Blue

The aging man doesn't pull the string;
lit, his room and its window stay blue
until dawn. As he works by himself, from

midnight on, everything is a challenge.
His pool of light leans quietly against
the dark around it, the books edging slowly

their remembered way off the shelves. Poets
in books bark orders at words, this hour.
They hit at their ankles where young animals

only want to play. Blue curtains survive
at the window, barely; if he pulled the lamp's
string, curtains would be black and shapeless.

Blue would move outdoors, into the street,
to rest with snow. There women and men
wait in the quiet glow of the city's

random windows. They are alone or
asking questions of their lovers, or
praying that frail relatives will survive

or else will die tonight. To pray at all
is what he prays for; to cover the window
or turn out the light, forget the line on

which colour moves. Blue cannot be the gist
of his heart alone. An absolute number stalls
in the empty air that moves in the empty walls.

Today a Blue Bowl

If it cracks, it is only a bowl.
No lesson to be learned. Carelessness

is nothing. At least not now, not here.
Think of a place it could matter, and

something as rich and thick as this
sauce is not what the bowl would hold

in its cup. Everything would be thinner.
You would need a month of brewing bark

to taste it. This elegant blue bowl
would never have been painted—it would

be here by accident, or treasured, won
in some adventure. And it would be holding

water, if there were such a thing as rain.

Bull Island

So that I made a poem of Bull Island, he died there.
Long ago, and stoically, with a slow and set expression

that hid his ultimate purpose: the ellipsis of his
worn breathing; the sunned-upon lines of his shrinking

body, the wounds of which were brown, yellow, or grey
before his eventual full stop. Kind and sure as a gesture

made on the city streets years before, a tanned smile
that was the artless part of wooing not just a young woman,

but the wife she would become. Waiting for her husband
to die on Bull Island, she hung decorations as always.

He had not told her he would die. The ending surprised him
also. Light in winter, even through bony tree limbs, is

too light. The sun this particular winter, at least
just now, unnecessary as science, its elucidation

a petty rewording of what he learned through his failing
body. She knew much later, but long before his bones were

found in spring. Years after, in a book, and in a story
by my mother, he was mentioned. And now, as every young man,

I am quick to believe. He died before Christmas, private, hurt,
on an island called Bull, as he was, by other men back then.

I walk into the shower to wash myself in steam. Words come
as I clean. There's no trace of sun on my body. I know he did

not die for me to write this poem. I cannot even pretend
my body may be wild. I scrub coffee off my tongue. My teeth

are too white. So I have, warm and clean, imagined a man just
to kill him, imagined a man named after the land, imagined

it was possible to be fair to him. When I close my eyes
in the unnatural deluge, I imagine I might keep this body, pale

as it is, out of the poem. Open the window. Let in the wind.
The grey limbs of trees can hide nothing from December.

December

Any moment
                we fear lucid
                                  questions. And people
with sorry eyes,
                everywhere. Dying
                                  men stare at the floor
and try not to
                shake. People
                                  comb their hair
to come here.
                They sleep in plastic
                                  chairs, afraid to
miss one final moment.
                The only young
                                  man in a wheelchair
smiles, so we must
                look outside:
                                  dull grass elbows
through snow.
                Some snow;
                                  it mimics dust.
It apes disease.
                You cannot draw
                                  a line there,

and expect a revelation—
            her paper body
                            lingers—*what is*

a moment?
            the television asks.
                          Just tell me where

you keep the clean
            gowns. I'll redress
                        her myself.

The Arrangements

We were on an even keel, keeping it
all together, as they say. With all

the well-wishers gone or going.
Now with these boxes and framed

photos of dark smiles—the heart's jargon is quickly
understood—this happens:

a picture of my four-year-old
mother holding a fish—anger and

confusion in her eyes—makes sense;
I have also been angry at

and confused by a dead fish
of all things. A black and white smell

on a string. A thing.

Asquith 18 km

At his desk, he can see the sign.
There is a small graveyard at the corner

of two roads and the sky crawls with cowards
in the shape of arcing birds. He wrote a book

about tumours. Silence. First his mother's, then
his father's. A warm elision stretches memory and

lives in the smell of baking bread, or
oil and dust. There is an empty lock, the metal ghost of a key.

The heart continues, collecting its things, offering
its limbs to old clothes. There is a cough from the lawyer

down the hall. The little graveyard sits
under holes in the clouds, with a few stubborn trees.

The car door doesn't make a sound as it closes.
He wrote a book about tumours. As the heart trundles

down the stairs with its kit, no one bumps into it.
There is no jostling at all. Poplars fidget in the air.

Witness to private, wordless shows, they guard nothing.
Silence. The stones, the monuments,

the wooden crosses. He coughs now, to steady himself. Down
the hallway is a little graveyard, a book about

tumours, the sky crawling with dead parents, the arc
meant for something more youthful than trees.

That Old Silver Ford

When my father let me drive that truck
I'd go and pick you up. We were young
and lapped at everything we touched
like a flood.

We drove down that old road, sometimes,
in the summer, when we were brown and thin
as animals; through the break in the trees to the clearing
where we watched the sky. And there
we were: pressed
to the ground by something simple
as colour—the colour blue
and the scent of green and you
and I two snakes shedding skin
in the dust, red
to red until the wind comes.

Home on the paved road, the windows down,
the hot prairie air is turned cool
by our speed.

Green Lawn, Under the Trees, a Cemetery Across the Street

Sitting on the stoop with a cigarette, calling
the dog and shaking keys in my holey pocket,

I wait for a sign she is making her way
back—a smile from this city's strangers, a quick bark,

the dark flash of her shadow behind the fence, before
she runs through the gate. Behind me, my children

marry, because we're moving in a week
and while packing I found a black suit for a four-year-old

boy, a six-year-old's white dress. Their solemn rehearsals
mythologize their past—they pretend to be

their mother and their father. I have heard them talking.
I don't know where they learned their lessons. No sign

of the dog; I will have to gather the children
and walk. Their mother is across the street lying

in a one-year-old hole, and I don't want to walk,
this tiny bride on one side, her still-learning groom

on the other. They will say the dog is lying on the lawn
above their mom. She won't be. But we will

wait, and see.

Still Life, Fixing the Mazda Pickup

The father tells the son next time
                         call when it's night, never
mind the time difference.
       He should be outside building an ark, or digging
a hole to catch the rain, or both.

             There was a time when his father wouldn't speak.
Now he describes everything he sees.

∽∽∽

There is a blue truck to fix. The mechanics are easy, logistics
too, except for money.
       So the father takes his time reciting long lines about how
simple engines used to be—there was no way
                 to diagnose the mechanical with software and
error codes; you knew by listening
       to the working machine. But this
                         little truck, despite so little
rust, is old, but won't make a sound.
       He's been at it three days.

The only thing left is the starter.
            Anyway, his hands have grown wider not longer.
                        They don't
feel the cold but delicate movements are
            beyond them. He's afraid he's lost

interest in the unmaking and making, the dark hands and oil,
                              the hard crawl under and back out.

                            ༄༄༄

Today, in this conversation, voices move
                  without even the need for hung wires. Even now,
I can't imagine where the words go
            without worrying there's a virus or worm shot through
my brain and that's why I forget
            what's been said.
                                        No immunity.

I know what he means: men don't come home from work anymore
with hair oiled and parted, with long sleeves in summer, rolling papers,
tin lunch boxes, reused waxed paper, a tin of tobacco by the sugar
bowl on the table and
                         you know what he means too.
There is a Nintendo with cigarette burns on a low shelf in our own garage.

The garage is heated, maybe for the dog to live in during winter.

And if the snow were heavy, it would sit
                       impossibly thick on the black wires
                       that used to span the poles. The wires always
seemed loose,
         they needed stretching, tightening,
                               but engineers have reasons
my eyes can doubt.

                            ༄༄༄

So even now, with the cables in ditches, I am afraid of the cold. You're not.
                                        I am the one

calling my father, he is the one talking about the old truck.
                                We all know this isn't a love poem.

Some things are used for storage and we know that.
Some things we hold so closely we can't see.
                        He is rebuilding a machine. He and I know
        what it means, so when I hear him
smash the window in the background, I want to
                        leave the phone on the concrete floor

and find you. *I better go,* he says—the father, I mean—
                                and *there's glass all over.*

He does what the son is accused of, avoids exclamation.

You do the accusing, but not now.   Now we don't.

Ghazal for Ross Leckie

The worn man holds a parcel, torn
from the ribs of winter.

There are laws about currency conversion.
There's a large book about everything.

Trying not to raise suspicion, I asked
about the standing water, the night-time smoke.

Out here, alphabets do not work.
Numbers make even less sense.

I would prefer not, he says, swinging
some imaginary chain, the band's heat behind him.

Second Opinion

The doctor was by to see you.
Make of it what you will, he said,
folding his arms. You were away.

Doctors don't look like doctors anymore.
The neat young man by your bed
looked thirsty. In the heat, he took a glass of water

from your pitcher. He explained your
silence as he sat where I could see:
everybody wants a second opinion. Where were

you? You might have been dead. There are things
that happen, he said through his sweating
smile, a person cannot or will not believe. He

got up to leave. I saw my dumb round eyes
in the glass as he crossed to the door.
How can you trust a doctor like that?

over this emergency

Seattle

I've never been there. She says
I have to go. The light here
is simple and hot. Nothing left
to cool us; the wind is spent.

The night here comes late.
Late is not soon enough, when
she paints her nails and sweat
drips like water down her side.

On the street it's worse.
She lies back. The city's too green.
My pulse waves slowly with her
closed eyes. The scent of her polished

toes hangs, sweet and impaired,
in the air. I'll take the water that
beads on her throat. Before she
can speak, before her drawn out

heart can beat again, before she's
right, and we leave. I will find the
words, in this living heat. I will open
her blushed wet mouth, and speak.

This Is a False False Mark

There is a book a stranger reads. I know
from her eyes it is *The End of Everything* but
its spine says *You Are Not Alone*

The stranger is a wife, the silence in the kitchen is
a metaphor for this end of civilization as sure as any
end of the road—

This place in the neighbourhood, for instance, where he was
just this morning, watching the black dog sniff
its black edge for what—some blood spilled long ago, some
excrement, something properly libidinal
that would become decay, some faded enunciation of mortality—no,
nothing so grand, and that was the problem:
he missed his childhood belief in large things.

He wanted to be able to say
all the things he could say
                            he could believe
in a broken heart, for instance, but age had shown
him: it was not an extraordinary condition,

I am all for ambiguity as long as it's clear that's what it is; I would
like it split down the middle like some kind of dove exclaiming its
dovesong each; half a beak but the whole song   times two
    That's what Solomon taught me, that's what the river running
wet salesmen through these cold mountains means, that's what her
grinding teeth as she sleeps, etc.

But your hero's arms had nowhere to go and the things you said
never made sense—I wanted wells of green tea, 800-thread-count

Egyptian air to breath and huge unfillable sockets and you whispered instead a litany of obvious things: the end of time, the depths of the ocean, the height, sincerely, of the moon, the moon of all things which, as we gathered ourselves into ourselves and made the trip out to the edge, as I say, we didn't need to think of, we didn't need to say . . .

this kind of thing is impossible because
there is a cold earth that spins by my walking
    there is a thin wire I know that's strung tight
        there is a dark sky that lights by my waking

all that is so, and yet, in this small office
one simple thought returns and returns again
    that I was outside one afternoon and missed
        you there, late in the day, where the pavement
            ends, and there we are, uncarred,

disautomobiled, even the sounds of this
earth, reaching us exactly where we stand
in the volunteer canola as it trembles
when the pavement ends and our idea of
a bird collapses like feathers held together
by air imploding in your absence
gathered later, when there is a need for song.

And now, she takes the time
    to sit down and cry
over this emergency—
    the small pad, its
very large pencil and
    enormous eraser

—while the world
    around her is desperate
and *clingy* if you want
    to know the truth

    she sits and sobs
magnificently, plus quietly,
    plus beautifully, warmly,
musically, if you must
    know the truth, finally.

Prairie Realism

The inherited hero
that I have also, mistakenly,
killed, embarrasses us all;
he just goes on. He will not begin
to die. He wants to be
the one exception,
to hang himself again
in trees that don't exist, or
burn into the earth
watching a grassfire, or
freeze when his heart cannot
seek warmth in these pages.

Murder can happen
in a flat land. Cities can.
Fast surviving women with happy
exteriors and interiors.
Landscape is the scope of
teachers and preachers, not heroes.
They can be killed too, let's say
in a room on the 29th floor,
a ravine, or a street,
Bay or Bloor. They can be killed
any time of day; but it's night
time for the prairie hero.

Ghazal

Somewhere out in the sprung world
birds are busy among themselves.

Hidden, as always, the power supply waits
under dyed metal skin for a technician.

The doors swung open, then closed.
You were in the middle of a joke.

During this precise war we were ready;
where are the children running like blood?

Now, softly, his old plaid shirt, waving
from the line—one arm escaped, one hanging on.

God Help Me

This is to say that death has been
undone. Its undoing
has been beauty.

The fallen bodies are rising up
again. Slender women are
reviving them.

This is to praise the necrophiliacs.
One moment follows on
the next and

dead men need love too. I will be
one soon enough. God
help me when

my regrown heart splashes through
a body long incapable
of holding it.

God help me when my lucky corpse
meets you.

They Meet Each Other in Airports

How long were you making these plans?
I meant to call, they say, not remembering they *had* called,

but had nothing to say.
What is the weather like there? Does it matter?

You are dressed in clothes you seldom wear.
You, with your bright bottle of water and reckless necklace,

rub your naked hand, with its dark nails, once across your throat.
Mouthing simple words, voices become terribly discrete.

And I thought so, too, long into the night.
I will never descend, I thought.

I am here in the dark, with my new strangers,
forever. This thing my own wife does in her sleep

beside me—is it habit?
Will someone miss it?

Snow Storm on Nose Hill

Steel toes hold the cold.
Winter air cleans my lungs,
but my body's cramping up.

A distant train signals
something. Everything means
distance to me; I'm still.

The job is menial, our progress
inevitable. This thirtieth winter
is no sign, and neither was

the twenty-ninth. Below this hill, the city
moves in lighted tics and pushes
nervous signals. What does this

require, this train sudden, moving
without thought? In the truck and
warming up, waiting for the wind to

stop, so we can see again, survey
this proposed church lot,
my face glows red and hot, long before

I feel my feet. The sky calms,
the air stretches, again we can
see. Our tracks in here are gone.

How Are We Betrayed?

Write a poem about the sound of water being poured into a glass while a man stutters and struggles to get the name Julia out. When the poem is finished, don't save it, because the telephone rings and your mother must have a ride to emergency. Leave the door unlocked because your wife forgot her key on the table beside her breakfast plate and you were staying home, doing the dishes, and writing. See your mother in the lobby, hurry up the walk to her door. Don't scold her for not waiting. Smile despite the pain in her glossy eyes and the quick makeup, the backwards eyebrow. Smell the perfume, ignore the urine underneath it.

                                                      Hurry home this time even though she lies under her blankets. She's wet at the edges of her thin hair. Be thankful the drugs let her sleep, watch her for a minute breathe, but hurry home this time because your wife needs the car. Be thankful because the poem is still there on your screen and this is how your eyes are fresh: why the name Julia and will she wait for the man to say her name or will she drink the water watching his pushing mouth and his abandoned eyes only to sigh and lower the glass to the oak table before leaving? Write a poem about the silence that follows his last terrible word, about the empty glass placed *carefully* on a wooden desk. Or is it *quickly*? *Is* it empty?

My Case

Our future child sleeps, hungry
in his wagon. He won't make a sound
but we can see it on his face.

The shutters in the other room clap,
or do what they can. The door moves
in and out. In fear of this baby

dying. I am too unsteady
to haul his toy carriage
behind me, to plead my case before

the butcher, groggy on his day off,
for food, for grease, for please something,
God, to eat—in this fear I stop

believing in a baby; a grown man
or woman can stand to lose. The concrete
walls of our house age smoothly. Quiet.

Winter comes and goes and wood pores
relax, stretch, creak. My body fights warily
in the early darkness when love wheels

round like a tricycle under a blanket. My eyes
come open. I need to breathe. Quickly, I say, come
now. I believe. Say what you need.

With His New Tooth

Listen. I cannot survive
here. The nude sky
embarrasses me.
I am human under

its enormous candor.
The scale of it, daily,
is a stubborn miracle.
We persist, but in

the shade of a parable
or a cartoon. My son,
with his new tooth,
can live in this world,

with his giddy heart
and sun-red face.
Standing here, there are
places I'll never reach.

Let this little man conquer—
too soon he will stand
on the naked earth,
diminished by his lessons:

our tongues are uglier
than the flesh we eat;
the blue world above
is a trick.

his perfunctory heart

Hinge

As she speaks her wrist bends
and pulls a cigarette to her mouth.

It's winter and the room will not get warm.
He watches her mouth speak, and there
in the kitchen, he takes a seat.

He knows the answer—eventually
her words will cause her to leave.
But all he can do is watch her thin arm bend
precisely at the wrist. If he could, he would pray.

She draws smoke from a cigarette and
breathes delicate words back with it. But he has always
been thick, and those words, he can't hear.

In another room of their house, somewhere, his heart
follows her words madly, beating
a blind guitar. But where he is,
something imagines a break in her spare body,
there, at its hinge, then pulls it back again.

What Is the Best Thing To do On A Hot Summer Day, Stopped For Road Construction?

What you *shouldn't* do is contemplate the eternal
verities and worry about the gas and should you
                                shut the engine off
and open all the windows
                   to hear whatever it is you may
hear and add the space between
                   the glass to the vast
still air of summer's heat and look
                   out as far as you can see to consider
also the gathering darkness and try to conjure
                   some cure, lift some spell from your too-
        seldom-used singing
voice to the shimmering light that seems
                 to rise, not fall.

The worst thing is to let your heart fall back
                   and imagine you're in your youth,
on a paving job in Drumheller,
               the longest day of the year.

It's sweet, the smell of fresh asphalt in the open air;
               it's like going home to the smell of turkey as
you come in from the cold
         on Christmas day, or the perfume of
                   the first woman you loved.

But recall again, especially, after
             the heat stroke—that before

it made you hurt, it made you stupid—
                        you knew it was the sun that burned,
and the black road you were making turned on you,
                              returning its heat in kind,
and you stood there, unable to speak, stupid, blind, until not
                                    falling, but slowly lowering
yourself onto its shoulder, as if
                  into cool water, but there was no water, was there?
I want to tell a secret now.
The ways the world can hurt are becoming
                  more obvious every day but unavoidable just the
same. I want to say there can be
    a word I know is coming, but thrills me
just the same—it is *impactful*, that is
        to say. But the world is coarse, it's bristling, as they
say. There are too many days
   when it just won't rain, so roll up the windows,
turn down the radio, listen to the wilderness
                  with the CBC underneath
and don't think of all the people gone: next thing you know
                        you're asleep in the sunshine and
that's pretty good. I think
        in the end you'll be awake, *listening to the chatter
each night of those who had survived
                the day* because
suddenly, startlement, a stolen word, the smile
                  that comes with it, or did, so just sit
and flex / you and your legs:

                    get out and stretch, stay a little
longer with the ones who love you.

This is the problem: we are here in our capsule, alone:
         the engines surround us, but
                 we are alone and the straight arrow of our journey,
this road, is for motion, not stasis—I got here by moving toward something else, which only ever *appears* closer, though it's not.
    I have been awaiting the arrival forever
                     and I hear in the voices, *listening
to the chatter each night of those who had survived the day* a tentative note just
above sorrow, even above

                   contentment, which, if we are

honest, can happen, *has* happened, so

above all don't narrow your sight to the scar on your hand on the wheel.

                         Are we the only

animal that feels regret? I saw a candle once blow out

            by the closing of a door, then burn

again with the movement of something within the dark room.

            It was never meant

as an experiment. Open the windows again,
                   let the heat seep in.

Plain Truck

The boy holds his own money and drinks in
what he can see over the one-ton's dash
on the ride into town. A sonofabitch says

something to his father as they walk
into the store, and the rumble does
not stop until they're back in the house

with his mother and she's crying, one
of his father's big hands resting easily
on her hip, and his muttering rolls into

new sound, until she believes him, and
he undoes her tied apron, forgetting the boy.
She turns and smiles with her wet face,

reties it, and the father's throaty vowel
breaks in laughter. They are surprised in the
warm kitchen. The boy too; mouth full of candy,

his wet laugh following his father's dark
eyes and the raw hands that cover them.

With My Own Shovel

I am making this tragedy every day.
It's not so bad. I name the assholes Keith
Something, after a big kid I never knew,

but who punched and kicked me daily.
It's such a thrill to watch him end up marrying
his sister, mixing things up, distorting

absolute truths, and so on, but people still love
him. In the end I always forget the bully or know
bullies do not burst onto the scene fully formed;

they're stick figures in another play, out of sight
somewhere. There is a guy I put in the background
with my father's name—he loves blood, he loves money—

trying not to show it. He kicks the shit out of this puppet
I made him. We hide it even from the audience.
In his perfunctory heart he wants to be a cowboy

—but the way he holds his face in his hands, and how
he can't even raise his head to kill food—he is unable
to sing for rain. My mother, of course, will have nothing

to do with it. After work I am back in the unpopulated
world of dirt and air, and surprised; there is little reaction
to me here, if any. I do the dishes, walk the dog.

I have the nagging sense that something is forgotten:
a key stuck in the lock like a knife through meat,
touching wood and ringing in the air; or love

that opened itself in every room of the house, until
in spring, when suddenly all exceptions were in play:
A boy held a green weed plucked from the sidewalk

—half of it was in his mouth, and he hated it, but didn't know why.

Ghazal for John Newlove

In the spirit of my ancestors, I look
from dirt to sky. It's hard to speak.

The kid, he gains wisdom every day.
He'll be down the road to school.

There's a red fire hydrant by our house.
We paint it, every so often, plain green.

Our destination is unclear. I've been
searching for Newlove. They haven't heard of him here.

The backhoe takes the road apart.
Hills have been piling up since dawn at the gate.

If You Look

Out in the lit yard rust wavers
by fenders and windows of the dull

red one-ton. My father sits with water
in a tin cup on the kitchen table

beside the plates with Saskatchewan's
old slogan. A screwdriver held without

thought rests on his leg. He's used
all his tricks. His eyes are closed—

normal, but the neighbours think he's waiting
for a stroke. Or would, if they were

here. The yard is bare with yellow grass.
Halfway down the road to Perdue, a man

younger than my father's paid good money
for this last truck. An old story:

the tool falls, he wakes up quickly,
but he's not moving to the city.

February 15, 2009

/who decides the mending of the fence has material as well as spiritual consequences? You are the one who feels each sliver in the skin should be your neighbour's.

Is it still Winter? you want to ask, because when the world is covered every few days

with such blank, wide, lawns, a man not believing in God can still believe in something to stand on along with empty beginnings.

That's how we want it now. So I have the appropriately ironic stance toward the lawn I know is under   the blank page before me, but it will be me who steps into it. I will be the one who thinks by this stepping to reveal the verities—stumble upon them, say, hoping they are not:

this page is so big today; this sky is so wide; where did she go— meaning: I am alone and afraid in this big world; meaning: I want to find some sign in the blue; meaning: the last woman I loved, where is she?

> The last time I saw her she ate
> cold shrimp from a white bowl. It was
> cold. I held her ceramic blue cat,
> knowing I was not good at fragility,
> and the bones in my hands hurt. I
> couldn't feel what I held. I didn't
> know where we went from there. Me
> on a plane, I guess. What about her?

But because it comes from above I can't know *exactly* what snow is.

I will be the one who steps into it, with more difficulty daily, my body more eloquent in its transmission of details down limbs to my brain, my heart more open to its own shortcomings, asking forgiveness as it shovels its heat more awkwardly.

> Are you the sinner that killed a black dog in your last book? Are you the one now, standing in the new snow with your hurtful plans

> Yes. I know. But don't take these gestures personally.

> For my next trick I kill also children, also forests, also everything concrete and steel must be destroyed. I may keep the glass its musical way of dying.

Poetry is the closest thing to silence, which alone on earth is as close as we get to [heaven]. If I could make the absence pink or brown I would. If I could make it skin, that is.

But no, I've chosen to be alone, with you, able to hear only myself, though I listen for you:

> And the second person can only respond. The snow has removed all signs, and under, it's ice. Stand as still as you can. We follow our empty tracks out to your deserted

parents' house, and, in the door,
quickly forget all of this.

I open each page, etc.

And in the past they made marble, orchestrated scores of musicians and even, in more ancient days, built cities or, at least, churches

What did I feel, leaning in the shadows of such tall buildings? What did I feel, escaping at night the brutal meanderings of a species pretending toward progress, or slouching, or breathing deeply, sleeping in the sunshine? The humans that did all humans do. Was I

The Final Poem

I guess the strategy for this one is
    to mark the path somehow;
    to singe the hair off the meat;
    to part the largest part of the sea;
    to work the nut snug, and hang by my arms, legs
        swinging, testing all I've built
    to stop a moment, wait and listen—is someone
        catching up or have I fallen behind?
    to speed over all the holes that scare me,
        never looking down
    to make up one black dog, one old man, to pretend
        the silence between them illuminates

I guess the reading gets its own work done
    it celebrates the end of the book
    it casts its shadow on the backward path
    it lets a machete dangle at the end of a tired arm while
        its brain flashes one more signal—we're not out of
        the jungle.
    it resides on the edge of town, quietly, in a cheap motel,
        waiting for the next party
    it worries its way into the next book, looking for connections,
        hooking up with a prime minister, still dying
    in the still drying concrete
    it hands its ticket to the first person in a uniform
    it marches through the doors and right up to the podium
    it speaks as if it must apologize
    it shrugs on a linen suit and prepares for life in the sunshine

1984 F150

has the exact features
of an ancient myth. The body is
the vehicle.

      Meat and potatoes on the stove.
Slats of weak light fall
on the table. The final offer. Smiles
divulge.

    I'm grateful
I never had a horse to shoot or sell.
The vehicle is the body. Mine is flippant;
gadgets buzz and whir under skin,
blur words. Once, the sun
did nothing but flatter.

I will not apologize again
for the dead truck in winter. I can still bend
at the waist, stand straight
shortly after waking.

The inevitable occurs daily
to the body. Broken ribs, trouble
ascending a hill, stains that embarrass
everyone. Death works
its way into every deal. Glazed
carrots relax in their white bowl.

ACKNOWLEDGEMENTS

The italicized quotes in "What Is the Best Thing To Do on a Hot Summer Day, Stopped for Road Construction" are from Jorie Graham's "Spoken from the Hedgerows", *Overlord*, NY: Ecco/HarperCollins, 2005, 41.

The italicized quotes in "Dec. 12, 2007" are from Leonard Cohen's "Poem", *Selected Poems 1956-1968*. New York, NY: Viking, 1970. 30.

The poems in this manuscript have appeared in the following:
"Asquith, 18 km" and "Today a Blue Bowl" in *echolocation*

"A Black and White Photograph,","Obviously," Last Summer in Rosetown", and "Bull Island" in the chapbook *Bull Island* (Gaspereau, 2004)

"Blue" in *Green Hills Literary Lantern*

"Obviously" and "Bull Island" in *The Fiddlehead*

"Plain Truck" and "August" in *Windsor Review*

"If You Look" in *The Antigonish Review*

"They Meet Each Other in Airports", "Spectacular", "The Complicated Mawkishness of My Daily Walk Home", and "Still Life, Fixing the Mazda Pickup" in *Ottawater*

"Hinge", "This Morning", and "Dead Song" in *Missing Jacket* and *Speak!* (Broken Jaw, 1997)

"Nothing Broken" in *Bywords* and *Good Reports*

"Fend" and "With My Own Shovel" in *Prairie Fire*

"Green Lawn, Under the Trees, a Cemetery Across the Street" in *Rocksalt* (Mother Tongue, 2008)

"This Is a False False Mark", "We're All Invited", and "What's the Best Thing to Do on a Hot Summer Day Stopped for Road Construction?" broadcast on CBC radio's *Daybreak South*

Thanks to the following people for their contributions to the long composition of the poems in this book: Sheri Benning; Roger Bird; Theo Bohn; Sarah Den Boer; Robert Hogg; Melissa Houghton; Jake Kennedy; Michael Kenyon; Stuart Konyer; Robert Kroetsch; Jim Larwill; Ross Leckie; John Lent; Christopher Levenson; Rob McLennan; Rocco Paoletti; Trish Pennie; Klause Pohle; Chris Pollard; Lee Ann Roripaugh; James Spyker; Ross Taylor; Malcolm Todd; and Craig Carpenter.